Up North MICHIGAN

PHOTOGRAPHY BY TOM BARRAT

NARRATIVE BY SARAH MORAN MARTIN

Copyright © 2023 by
Tom Barrat

All rights reserved. No part of this book may be reproduced in any form without written permission of the copyright owners. All images in this book have been reproduced with the knowledge and prior consent of the artists concerned and no responsibility is accepted by producer, publisher, or printer for any infringement of copyright or otherwise, arising from the contents of this publication. Every effort has been made to ensure that credits accurately comply with information supplied.

First published in the
United States of America by:

Tom Barrat
Walloon Lake

ISBN: 979-8-218-11732-0

10 9 8 7 6 5 4 3 2 1

(opposite)
Petoskey Sunset

(frontispiece)
Wequetonsing Association, Harbor Springs

(jacket front)
17 Sailboat on Walloon Lake

(jacket back)
Lake Campfire at Dusk *(top)*,
Pierhead Lighthouse, Petoskey *(bottom)*

Book design by:
Sara Day

Printed in China

A breathtaking jewel in Michigan's crown, Up North is a place like no other. Water is everywhere and water defines it. Michigan boasts more than 3,000 miles of fresh-water shoreline, more than any other state in the U.S.

The Tip of the Mitt, as it is sometimes called, brims with pristine lakes, rolling hills, wildflower-dotted forests and charming towns. Three of them—Petoskey, Harbor Springs and Charlevoix—are featured in this book, as well as the lakeside resort communities of Harbor Point, Bay View, Bay Harbor and Walloon Lake. It is a treasured destination for people from around the globe.

Odawa and Ojibwe Native Americans first settled here in lakeside fishing villages. They bent young saplings to mark trails and provide direction, especially in deep winter snows. This practice gave rise to the name Crooked Tree *(L'Arbre Croche)*, currently found on Petoskey's arts center, a well-known bakery and a resort nestled in the curve of Little Traverse Bay. European settlers arrived in 1715 and built a fort where Mackinaw City now stands. French trappers, hunters and missionaries followed and the fur trade and farming flourished.

Workers felled vast northern forests as growing cities whetted the Midwest's insatiable appetite for lumber. In 1873, the advent of railroad and steamships forever changed Up North's face. People arriving by train and boat escaped oppressive summers in Detroit, Chicago and other cities. Notable among them was renowned author Ernest Hemingway and his family, who summered on Walloon Lake.

In 1876, local Methodists organized the Bay View Association—a chautauqua, or church camp—on Little Traverse Bay. It prospers to this day with colorful Victorian-era homes and a vibrant arts scene. Industrialists and lumber barons built fancy lakeside homes, ironically calling them *cottages*. Many still stand, the water their sparkling front yard.

From its million-dollar sunsets, brilliant fall colors and heavy snowfall to a wealth of outdoor activities, rich culture, trendy shops and restaurants, Up North enchants all who visit and live here. Photographer and Walloon Lake resident Tom Barrat captures Up North's splendor and spirit that I, as a fellow Walloon Laker, have come to know and love so well.

— Sarah Moran Martin

Ignatius Petosega Statue

Overlooking Little Traverse Bay, this imposing bronze statue of Chief Ignatius Petosega, created by sculptor Pietro Vinotti, was erected in 2005. Petosega, Petoskey's namesake, was a local merchant and Odawa Nation chief. Son of a French fur trader and a Native American woman, his name, loosely translated, means *rising sun*.

Petoskey Pierhead Lighthouse
(top and bottom)

The Petoskey Pierhead Lighthouse, with its signature red stripe, stands 40 feet tall at the end of the Petoskey breakwall. The flashing red light is a beacon for the Petoskey City Marina. Michigan has 129 lighthouses dotting its shores, the most of any state in the U.S.

Petoskey Breakwall Walkway (top)

Originally built in 1899 and vastly shored up in 2009, the Petoskey Breakwall juts from the Petoskey Marina into Little Traverse Bay. It protects the marina and shoreline from severe beatings often inflicted by churning water, storms and ice. Those walking on the breakwall often get doused with waves.

Pierhead (bottom)

Fall never fails to put on a colorful show Up North, with the region's wealth of deciduous hardwoods. Typically ablaze from late September through October, these trees, in their autumnal glory, light up the landscape with the breakwall, lighthouse and Little Traverse Bay in the distance.

Bayfront Park *(top)*

Once an industrial area, this 25-acre public park borders Little Traverse Bay with more than a mile of shoreline. In warmer weather, the park is alive with visitors. They flock to fly kites, play on the expansive lawn, lounge near the water and linger in chairs or hammocks to watch the sun slip below the horizon.

Ed White Softball Field *(bottom)*

On many a summer's day, cheers and the thwack of a softball echo from the Ed White Softball Field in Bayfront Park. Men and women play fast and slow-pitch games and tourneys here. Ed White coordinated many of them during his 40-year stint as Michigan Amateur Softball Association commissioner.

Bayfront Park

Bayfront Park's craggy shoreline is a common destination for those seeking Up North's signature Petoskey stones. The park features a 144-slip marina, a playground, the Ed White tournament-class softball field, a waterfall, City Hall, a fishing pond, a seasonal snack bar and ample parking, among other amenities.

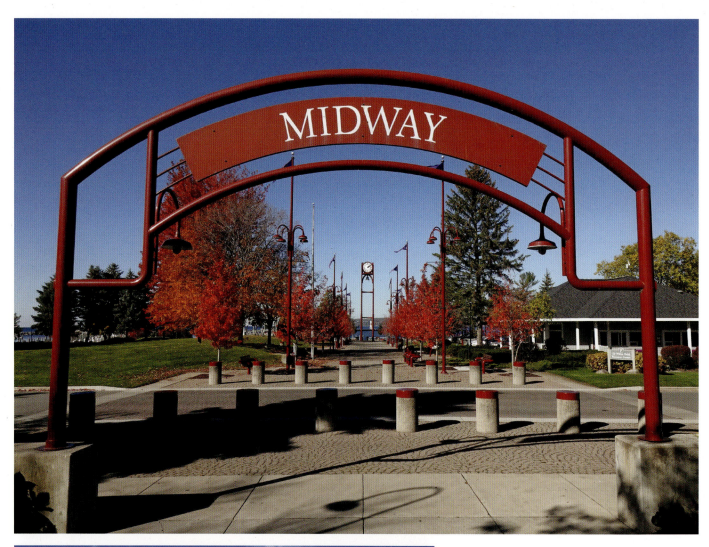

Petoskey Midway *(above)*

The Midway provides access to Petoskey's famous Gaslight District shopping area, once called the Midway, via a concrete pedestrian tunnel from Bayfront Park. Cyclists and pedestrians use the Midway to access the Little Traverse Wheelway, a 26-mile, rail-to-trail paved bike path following former railroad tracks. It starts in Charlevoix and ends in Harbor Springs.

Bayfront Park Clock *(left)*

A proud sentinel at the Petoskey Marina, the Petoskey Clock Tower was erected more than 30 years ago. It is a replica of the original clock adorning the Emmet County Courthouse. Namesake Robert Emmet was an Irish nationalist who never set foot here. The name honors the many Irish immigrants who settled in the area.

Lifeboat at Bayfront Park *(top)*

Snatched from its mooring and sunk in a 2020 storm, this 20-person lifeboat from the freighter *J.B. John* was recently restored by merchant mariner Lon Calloway. One of the Great Lakes' most historic vessels, the *J.B. John* was owned by Petoskey Portland Cement and plied the Great Lakes for nearly 60 years.

Bayfront Park *(bottom)*

Bayfront Park tucks up against Little Traverse Bay, from west of Ingalls Avenue to south of Belle Avenue, and from U.S. 31 east of Stuart Avenue. Though not officially a swimming beach, Bayfront Park visitors often wade in Little Traverse Bay to hunt for Petoskey stones, shells and other lake-life souvenirs.

East Park *(above and left)*

High atop a grassy bluff overlooking Little Traverse Bay, scenic East Park is often teeming with visitors eager to catch the sun dipping below the western horizon of Lake Michigan. Views of the water are all-encompassing and breathtaking. Advertisers, at times, take full advantage of the park's expansive views, using this dramatic scene as a backdrop for car commercials.

East Park is free and open to the public. Located at the eastern edge of Bay Harbor, it skirts part of the 26-mile Little Traverse Wheelway. The park offers a large playground, public restrooms, picnic tables and a covered pavilion that can be rented for events, all overlooking Little Traverse Bay.

Bayfront Park West and the Wheelway
(above and right)

Bayfront Park West, another green lung fronting Little Traverse Bay, adjoins Bayfront Park. The paved wheelway follows a trail around the bay that existed prior to 1900. Now it connects with the North Western State Trail, accessible off M-119 outside Harbor Springs. The trail's paved and crushed limestone surfaces run 32 miles to Mackinaw City.

Waterfall in Bayfront Park

Near the end of Bayfront Drive is this man-made waterfall with unimpeded views of Little Traverse Bay. Water from drainage ditches above cascades into a creek that empties into Lake Michigan. It is a popular site for selfie photos, weddings and other events. Stairs take visitors to Sunset Park, high atop the bluff.

Bear River Walk *(top)*

A pedestrian bridge near Petoskey spans the 15-mile Bear River, originating at Walloon Lake's Foot. The river winds its way east and north, eventually emptying into Little Traverse Bay. A scenic 1.5-mile path hugs the river and is popular for walking, biking, cross-country skiing, snowshoeing, and other activities.

Bear River Walk and Bridge *(bottom)*

Built in 1930, the West Mitchell Street Bridge carries West Mitchell Street (US HWY 31) over the Bear River. Visitors can walk beneath the concrete structure to reach the Bear River Walk or downtown Petoskey (once known as Bear River). Artists and photographers often come here to capture its graceful arches.

Bear River Walk to the Bay (top)

The typically slow-moving Bear River flows through sylvan forests and tranquil farm fields on its way to a dam and Little Traverse Bay. Here it runs alongside the Petoskey Marina toward what many locals call *The Big Water*, aka Lake Michigan. The Bear River is the bay's largest tributary.

Bear River Valley Recreation Area (bottom)

The Bear River Valley Recreation Area offers a rolling paved path into Petoskey, with picnicking, covered pavilions, benches, barbecue grills and glimpses of the river beyond the trees. It also has ample parking and public restrooms. At its base, the recreation area connects with the Little Traverse Wheelway.

Cascading Bear River (opposite)

The Bear River picks up steam as it drops 75 feet, and plunges over rocks and a circa-1917 concrete dam at Lake Street before dumping into Little Traverse Bay. Spilling over the dam, the characteristic brown water mirrors hues from surrounding cedar forests. The area is frequented by avid fishermen and visitors alike.

Riverbend Park *(top and bottom)*

At one end of the Bear River Walk is scenic Riverbend Park. The park features a ramp-and-rail equipped skateboard park, volleyball and pickleball courts, a canoe launch and parking. Canoes and kayaks can often be spotted on the river. Closer to the bay is a quarter-mile kayaking course for thrill-seekers with rapids, swirls and a small waterfall when water is highest, usually during the snow-melt months of April and early May. Local garden clubs plant and maintain seasonal flower beds and butterfly gardens along the walk. Leashed dogs are welcome and, in some spots, can run unencumbered.

Salmon Fishing *(top and bottom)*

Fishing enthusiasts often flock to the Bear River to try their hand at catching salmon and steelhead trout, while visitors congregate to watch. Migratory fish run in the river and Petoskey Harbor, and more fish are stocked annually by the Michigan Department of Natural Resources. Favorite fishing spots are near the dam and where the river flows past the marina toward Little Traverse Bay. A boy proudly displays his catch on a summer's day. Salmon roe clusters (*bottom right*), which the fish expel, glisten in the sunlight. Usually eaten raw, the protein-packed roe is considered a delicacy by many.

Petoskey Marina *(top and bottom)*

A short walk from Petoskey's historic Gaslight District, the Petoskey Marina has moorings for approximately 150 boats during warmer weather. Numerous flower beds add vibrant pops of color until the marina closes October 1. Trees that dot the architectural landscape put on an autumnal show each fall.

Petoskey State Park *(opposite top)*

Located three miles northeast of Petoskey and six miles south of Harbor Springs, this popular public park hugs Little Traverse Bay. It encompasses over 303 acres with dunes, walking trails, camping, a snack bar, restrooms and picnic tables. The bay is the star here, with water stretching west as far as the eye can see.

Sand and Surf *(opposite bottom)*

Home to a pristine, mile-long beach with soft, clean sand, Petoskey State Park skirts Lake Michigan and is open year-round. Because it's at the easternmost point of Little Traverse Bay, beachcombers often find shells and hunt for increasingly elusive Petoskey stones. Canoes and kayaks can also be rented here.

Petoskey Stone Hunting

Michigan's sandy beaches are often dotted with shells and rocks, making them fertile ground for beachcombers. Many people enjoy hunting for Petoskey stones, a prized find. These stones are often polished and fashioned into a variety of popular decorative objects, including jewelry and paperweights.

Petoskey Stone Hunting *(top and bottom)*

The state stone of Michigan, the Petoskey stone is actually a fossilized coral. It is sometimes hard to find, but that does not deter rockhounds and beachcombers from scouring the area's beautiful coastline for these usually smooth-textured remnants of the Ice Age. Petoskey stones are unique to the Great Lakes.

Petoskey Skyline

The elegant spire of St. Francis Xavier Catholic Church, the city's tallest building, has long dominated Petoskey's changing skyline. Its bricks came from Boyne City and its rafters from felled local elm trees. Rooftops from Petoskey's Gaslight District poke through the trees on the left.

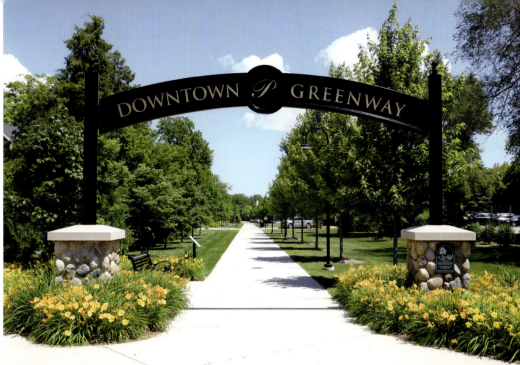

Downtown Greenway *(top and bottom)*

A generously wide pedestrian and bicycle pathway, the Downtown Greenway follows the route of a former railway through the heart of Petoskey and east toward Bay View. Cutting a swath through Petoskey's retail district on its way, the Greenway affords expansive views of Little Traverse Bay.

Downtown Petoskey *(opposite top)*

Surrounded by seasonal blooms, signage along US 31 welcomes all to the downtown area in Petoskey's signature Victorian style. Downtown Petoskey is comprised of a vibrant amalgam of shops, restaurants, the Perry Hotel, churches and other businesses, as well as several well-maintained parks.

Carnegie Library *(opposite bottom)*

A fine example of neo-classical revival style, the Carnegie Library is an iconic Petoskey landmark. Built in 1908, its construction was financed primarily by a $12,500 donation from Andrew Carnegie. Frequented by Ernest Hemingway during his residency, today it is listed on the National Register of Historic Places.

Petoskey District Library *(above)*

On East Mitchell Street, across from the Carnegie Library, is the impressive brick main building of the Petoskey District Library, which opened in 2004. Earlier, in 1989, the city purchased the former Michigan Bell building next door to expand the library, which was then incorporated into the new building's design.

Cutler's *(top)*

Anchoring a prominent corner downtown, Cutler's home and kitchen store is distinguished by its sunny yellow awnings and façade. First opened in Harbor Springs in 1965 by Bill and Jutta Cutler, it was later closed and reopened in Petoskey in the 1980s. Their daughter Carrie later joined the business.

City Hall *(bottom)*

Petoskey's City Hall anchors Bayfront Park and faces Little Traverse Bay, alongside the sometimes-rushing Bear River. The city's police and fire stations are also located next to City Hall. Petoskey is the county seat of Emmet County, one of Michigan's 83. Separate government offices are nearby.

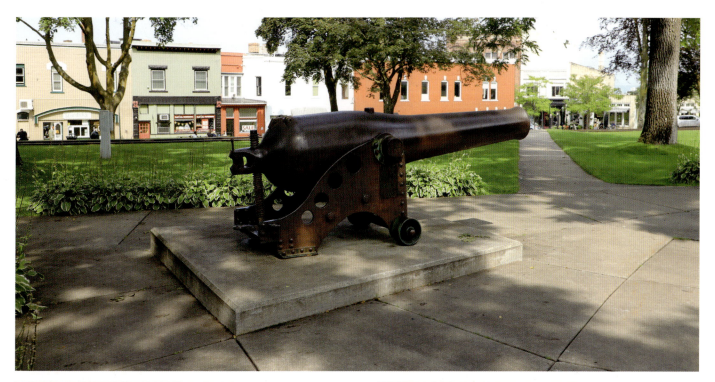

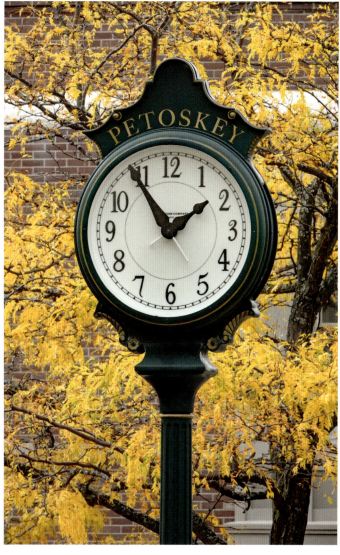

Farragut's Cannon *(top and above left)*

Farragut's Cannon came to Petoskey's Pennsylvania Park in 1905. A Dahlgren IX from the USS *Hartford*, it was used in the 1864 battle for Mobile Bay, Ala. Named for Admiral David Farragut, who helped gain Union control there, the cannon is now a popular selfie location and a delight for kids to climb upon.

Petoskey Clock *(right)*

A decorative sidewalk post clock adds to the charm of Petoskey's famous Gaslight District. A historic section of Petoskey's downtown, the Gaslight District lends itself to leisurely strolling, shopping and dining. Visitors and residents can browse more than 60 specialty shops lining its quaint and bustling streets.

Downtown Shops *(above and left)*

The Flora Bae Home *(above)* features artwork created by women and goods supplied by women-owned small businesses. The shop is owned by Michigan native Natalie Bae Luzon.

Housed in a historic 1876 structure, Grandpa Shorter's Gifts *(left)* has been family-owned since 1946. Shorter's is Petoskey's original souvenir shop and offers a treasure trove of Northern Michigan wares.

Gaslight District Shops *(above)*

Constructed between 1870 and 1930, many Petoskey buildings have been lovingly restored, retaining their unique Victorian ornamentation. Some are mixed-use with brightly painted exteriors housing shops and restaurants at street level, and offices and apartments above. These buildings line Lake Street in Petoskey's Gaslight District.

Chandler's *(right)*

Chandler's, a popular restaurant and wine bar, features an outdoor patio and a 4,000-bottle wine cellar. Located on the lower level of Symons General Store, it was once the Mole Hole, a beloved and dearly departed gift shop. A Saks Fifth Avenue store and later, the Toad Hall store, were once next door.

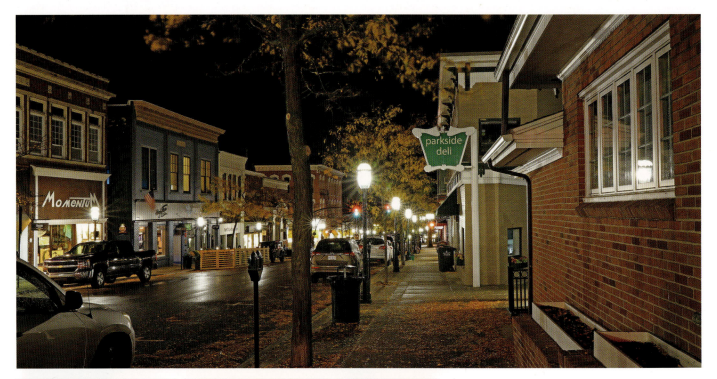

Petoskey at Night *(above)*

Petoskey's Gaslight District is more than 100 years old. Flickering gas lamps on slim posts line the streets, adding old-world vitality to a shopping district bursting with boutiques, restaurants, coffee shops, breweries, distilleries and other businesses. In the past, many shops would close during winter months and relocate to warmer locations, primarily in Florida.

East Mitchell Street *(left)*

East Mitchell Street is the main business thoroughfare in Petoskey. It is lined with shops, offices and eateries, some with outdoor dining when the weather warms. Atop Mitchell is a historic residential district where homes, large and small and of several architectural styles, are lovingly maintained.

Downtown Shops

Symons General Store *(above)* is housed in Petoskey's first brick building. With its distinct red hue and old-time ambience, Symons offers specialty foods from local and international purveyors. Palette Bistro *(below left)* is a popular restaurant and bar with impressive views of Little Traverse Bay. The old Hollywood cinema marquee *(below right)* still exists, though not the theater itself.

Kilwin's *(top)*

No trip to Northern Michigan would be complete without a visit to Kilwin's, a candy, fudge and ice cream shop established by Don and Katy Kilwin in 1947. As visitors watch, Kilwin's makes its own confections and ice cream at this facility near Bay View. Now a franchise, Kilwin's has more than 100 stores in 25 states.

Murdick's *(bottom left and right)*

Fudge shops, with their alluring aroma, are ubiquitous Up North. Begun in 1887 on Mackinac Island, Murdick's uses time-honored family recipes to make fudge, which is cooled and formed on marble tables. The surface gives the confection a unique texture and provides a stage for glimpses of how fudge is made.

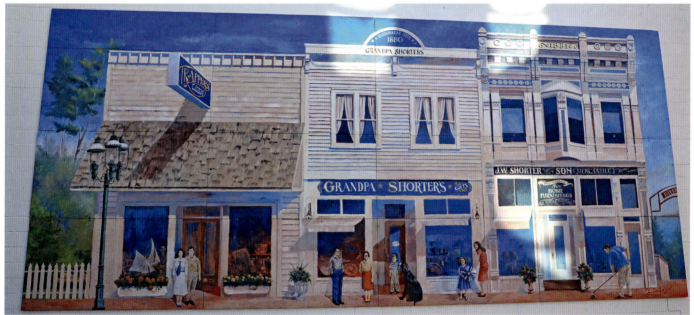

Artist Murals

A whimsical school of fish adorning a building near Kilwin's main store was painted by artist Amy Kent along with several students.

Bay City muralist Terry Dickinson created a row of busy shops *(above)* on the back of Grandpa Shorter's, as well as a delightful sidewalk scene *(right)* on a wall of the Sky's the Limit Flower Shop. It is one of the largest murals Dickinson has ever painted.

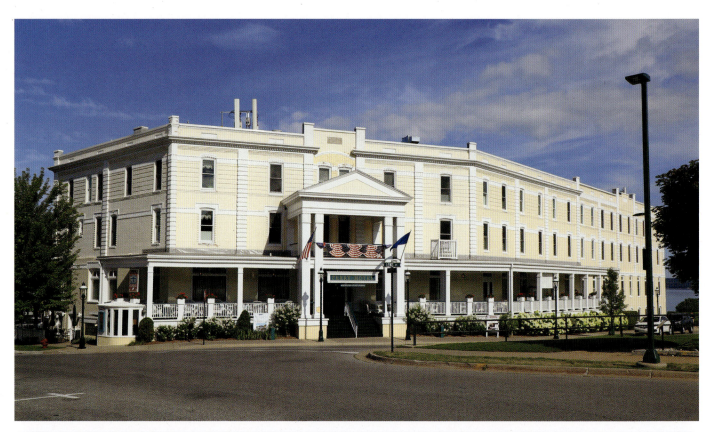

Stafford's Perry Hotel (top)

Petoskey's first brick hotel, the cream-colored Perry is the city's last remaining hotel from a bygone era of elegant lodging. Many of its 70-plus rooms offer magnificent views of Little Traverse Bay. The Perry has two restaurants and the popular Noggin Room, which often features live entertainment.

Odawa Casino (bottom)

Open since 2007, the Odawa Casino is owned and operated by the Little Traverse Bay Bands of Odawa Indians, who are among the area's original inhabitants. Designed by Leo A. Daly Architects, the casino, with its distinctive rooflines, and a hotel, cost $140 million. It is one of Emmet County's major employers.

Willson's Garden Center *(above)*

Opened in 1921 by O.D. and Myrtie Willson, this fifth-generation garden center on US 31 always puts on a lush roadside display during the growing season. Open seasonally, it offers annuals, perennials, shrubs and trees especially suited to the area's weather extremes.

Flatiron Building *(right)*

Built to accommodate the railroad right-of-way, Petoskey's late 19th-century Flatiron Building is one of several downtown structures that have unusual angular shapes. Others include the Perry Hotel, the former J.C. Penney building and Meyer Hardware. The Flatiron is currently home to Parkside Deli.

City Park Grill

City Park Grill, housed in one of Petoskey's oldest buildings, was once a men-only billiard hall and watering hole called The Annex. A special seat at the long wooden bar commemorates famed author and summertime Walloon Lake resident Ernest Hemingway, who lived in Petoskey following WWI.

Ernest Hemingway Plaques (left)

The Hemingway family, from Oak Park, Illinois, long vacationed during the summer on Walloon Lake. Ernest recuperated in Petoskey from injuries he sustained during WWI. He used Northern Michigan as the setting for his Nick Adams stories and *The Torrents of Spring* novella.

Ernest Hemingway Statue (right)

This bronze statue in Pennsylvania Park of a young Ernest Hemingway is based on a 1920 photo taken nearby. Depicted with a cane for support following his injuries during WWI, Hemingway is shown awaiting a train for Toronto, where he became a foreign correspondent for *The Star* and traveled extensively.

Pennsylvania Park *(above)*

A quaint gazebo featuring a graceful curvilinear tin roof is tucked beneath surrounding shade trees in Pennsylvania Park. Concerts are held at the gazebo each summer. *Art in the Park*, a juried fine-arts show, also takes place in the park every July. More than 100 artists display and sell their creations.

Pennsylvania Park *(top)*

Dormant tracks from the Grand Rapids and Indiana Railroad still exist in Pennsylvania Park and throughout much of Petoskey. The name changed to Pennsylvania Central Railroad in 1920. At its height, GR&I trains brought passengers and freight from Cincinnati as far north as the Straits of Mackinac.

Pennsylvania Plaza *(bottom)*

The original structure that was Petoskey's first train depot burned down in 1899 and was eventually rebuilt with brick. Tourists often took the train north to start their summer vacations. Home to various businesses over the years, Pennsylvania Plaza now houses an interior design firm and other offices.

Boyne Valley Vineyards (top)

Tucked between Walloon Lake and Petoskey off US-131 and recognized by a vintage 1952 Chevy truck often parked in front, Boyne Valley Vineyards is one of the area's newer vineyards and tasting rooms. Live music, wine and snacks are served up here, with heated igloos keeping visitors warm during winter.

Hay Bales (bottom)

A harbinger of cooler weather to come, hay bales often dot rolling farm fields at summer's end into early fall. Once hay is cut and dried, farmers roll it into bales, transport them to barns and use them for animal feed and bedding. Emmet County still has about 300 farms, most of which are family-owned.

Resort Pike Cidery & Winery *(top)*

South of Petoskey, Resort Pike Cidery & Winery sells sparkling and still wines and hard ciders in bottles, cans and on tap. An original barn on the property, lovingly restored, is now the tasting room. Hard ciders range in flavor from apple/blueberry and cherry/apple to an unusual pear-based version.

Petoskey Farms and Vineyard *(bottom)*

Depending on Up North's ever-changing weather, the area's wineries offer a wealth of tasting experiences. Petoskey Farms and Vineyard, east of Petoskey, welcomes visitors with Adirondack chairs and fruit-laden vines. The eighth largest grape-producing state, Michigan grows more than 50 different varieties.

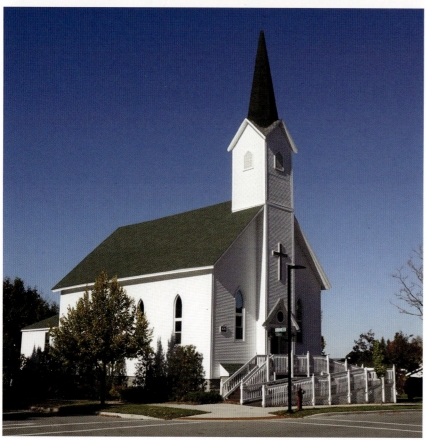

St. Francis Xavier Catholic Church *(above)*

At 183 feet tall, this imposing brick church is Petoskey's tallest point, and is visible from many places. Constructed at the start of 1903, the church replaces the original wood church, which had been moved earlier. Six artists painted the luminous interior walls. St. Francis X, as it's known locally, operates a school for children—kindergarten through eighth grade.

Emmanuel Evangelical Church *(left)*

Perched high atop a hill overlooking Little Traverse Bay, this church was one of Petoskey's first. Established in 1880 by German evangelical settlers, services and church documents were exclusively in German until church leaders added English in the 1920s. In 1975, they eliminated German from worship services.

St. Francis Solanus Indian Mission
(above and right)

This historic wooden mission, built in 1859, is the oldest surviving building in Petoskey and also one of the oldest in Northern Michigan. It is also Petoskey's first Catholic Church. A graveyard and white picket fence surround it. The historical marker is one of the few in Michigan that is printed in both the English and Odawa languages.

Mineral Well Park Pavilion *(opposite top)*

Petoskey has long been known for the quality of its potable water. At this site on the east side of the Bear River, several fieldstone wells and a bathhouse once stood where visitors could partake of the water's curative powers. Local architect C.H. Hansen designed this open-air pavilion, erected in 1917.

New Life Anglican Church *(opposite bottom)*

Over its nearly 100-year history, this beige brick church on State St. has housed a variety of denominations. An annex was added in 1979 for Sunday school rooms and a nursery. Located in a largely residential neighborhood, it became New Life Anglican in 2013.

Crooked Tree Arts Center *(above)*

Once the United Methodist Church, this colorful 1890 Gothic Revival building is now home to the Crooked Tree Arts Center. The center offers classes and events in the arts including fine art, music, dance, and theatre. It also sponsors the annual D'Art for Art fundraiser. It added a Traverse City campus in 2015.

Petoskey Bridge Club *(top)*

Recognized by its cupola and whimsical outdoor sign, the Petoskey Bridge Club hosts a rich roster of bridge classes, tournaments and other events for card enthusiasts. Teachers instill a variety of techniques and intricacies of this challenging game. Over 100 donors anted up funds to erect the building in 2009.

Meyer Ace Hardware *(bottom)*

This family-owned store on Petoskey's main drag offers more than nuts and bolts. It is well-known for gifts, kitchen items, Michigan-made goods and other wares. Like several in Petoskey, the Meyer building is angular and hugs tracks from the former GR&I railroad that once ran through adjacent Pennsylvania Park.

McLaren Hospital (top)

Known as Little Traverse Hospital, then Northern Michigan Regional Hospital, this 202-bed facility became part of Flint-based McLaren Hospitals in 2012. It serves 22 Northern Michigan counties and has a network of providers and specialty-care clinics. McLaren's Karmanos Cancer Institute is also at the hospital.

Little Traverse History Museum (bottom)

Once a depot for the now-defunct Chicago and West Michigan Railroad, the Little Traverse Historical Society turned the depot into a museum in 1970. It has a vast collection of maps, photos, Hemingway memorabilia and other items, many donated by residents. The museum overlooks Little Traverse Bay.

North Central Michigan College and Sculpture Garden

A two-year community college, North Central sits high atop Petoskey's rolling hills. Founded in 1959, it enrolls nearly 2,000 full- and part-time students. The Harris Gardens, named for benefactor Jack Harris, display nearly 30 sculptures, surrounded by landscaped gardens and paths.

Petoskey High School *(top)*

Petoskey High School and its adjacent Middle School are now located east of their original downtown location. The high school enrolls about 1,000 students. High-school athletes, known as the Petoskey Northmen, compete in a variety of sports and play football every fall at this state-of-the-art stadium.

Emmet County Fairgrounds *(bottom)*

This multi-use fairgrounds has a community building, equestrian center, grandstand and barns, all of which can be rented. It hosts a variety of events, including weddings, antique shows, ping-pong tourneys and fundraisers. The annual Emmet-Charlevoix County Fair is held here the third week of August.

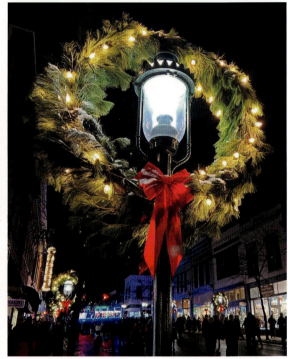

Holiday Open House

Petoskey merchants open their doors each first Friday in December to welcome holiday revelers. Santa kicks it off with a Christmas-tree lighting in Pennsylvania Park. The 40-member Petoskey High School Steel Drum Band offers a unique blend of Caribbean steel drum and contemporary music from an open-air trolley.

July 4th Parade (top and bottom)

A longstanding tradition Up North, Petoskey and neighboring towns host rousing parades, live music (including the Petoskey High School Steel Drum Band), food, fireworks and other events to celebrate America's independence. Sunrise Rotary Club of Petoskey and other organizations sponsor Petoskey's Fourth.

Ignatius Petosega Statue

The commanding silhouette of Ignatius Petosega presides over Little Traverse Bay in weather both fair and foul. In 1873, town leaders selected the anglicized *Petoskey*, in honor of the Odawa Nation chief and his family, as the new name for their growing community. In his hands he holds feathers and a peace pipe.

Land of Sunsets (top and bottom)

Petoskey has long been known as the *Land of the Million-Dollar Sunsets*. In late 1873, a reporter from Grand Rapids arrived by train just as the sun sank into Lake Michigan. Dazzled by the flaming skies, he coined the phrase and it stuck. Up North's spectacular sunsets are visible from many vantage points.

Holy Childhood of Jesus Catholic Church

Piercing the clouds and dominating Harbor Springs' skyline is the spire of the Holy Childhood of Jesus, the fourth church to stand at this site. From the late 1880s to 1983, it ran a controversial boarding school for Native Americans. Today, it hosts regular services and community events such as the fall Festival of the Book.

Harbor Springs Aerials (top and bottom)

Known as *Little Traverse* until it became Harbor Springs in 1880, this picturesque city on Little Traverse Bay hugs a sheltered bay that is considered the Great Lakes' deepest natural harbor. Named for numerous springs burbling into Lake Michigan, its year-round population of 1,200 swells substantially in warmer weather.

Little Traverse Lighthouse *(above)*

The U.S. government built this red brick lighthouse on the tip of Harbor Point in 1884. In 1896, it installed an 1,800-pound fog bell that clanged every 30 seconds in foul weather. The lighthouse was shuttered in 1963 and sold back to the Harbor Point Association, which undertook a renovation. It is not open to the public.

Harbor Point Association *(left)*

These stone pillars have long stood as sentries at the entrance of the private Harbor Point Association. Visitors must receive permission to enter at the quaint guard house. Owners park at Harbor Point's outer edge and either walk, bike or take horse-drawn carriages to the often expansive cottages here.

Harbor Point *(above)*

A longtime summer refuge for well-known industrialists whose families still own residences, Harbor Point was once called the Lansing Resort. The hamlet began when friends from Lansing, the state's capital, camped on this slender finger of land jutting into the bay. Residents built about 100 cottages, plus a hotel, boat- and bathhouses and a dock.

Pointer Boat *(right)*

Built by the Coast Guard in 1934, the *Pointer* once traveled between Harbor Springs and Harbor Point as a water taxi. Stafford Smith and Dudley Marvin of Stafford's Hospitality hired local boat builder Steve Van Dam to restore it. Now graced with a compass rose table, this wooden classic offers harbor and open-water tours.

Lyric Theatre *(top)*

A gleaming state-of-the-art movie theatre with three screens, the Lyric opened in 2016. Run entirely by volunteers, its name comes from a beloved nearby movie theatre that closed in 1981. Situated on Harbor Springs' Main Street, it is open year-round and shows first-run, classic and family-friendly flicks.

Ephraim Shay House *(bottom)*

Ephraim Shay, creator of the Shay geared locomotive, built this remarkable hexagonal house in 1892 and lived here with his wife. Both exterior and interior are clad in unusual stamped steel panels. Mary Cay Bartush Jones, who eventually owned the home, gave it to the Harbor Springs Historical Society in 2016.

Harbor Springs Homes (top and bottom)

Once a Native American village, Harbor Springs today is replete with expansive homes, many of them bordering Little Traverse Bay. Called *cottages* by locals despite their often huge size, many close during winter and reopen in warmer months as Harbor Springs' population swells with seasonal residents and tourists.

Wequetonsing *(top)*

Wequetonsing, *Head of the Bay* in Native American dialect, is a private association. In the 1870s, citizens donated 80 acres for a Presbyterian resort spearheaded by two Illinois businessmen. More than 100 homes were built, along with a dock, post office and golf course. A hotel was razed in 1964, making room for more.

Harbor Springs Homes *(bottom)*

Often called the *town of front porches*, Harbor Springs boasts many homes with wide porches graced with swings and vintage wicker furniture. Many open onto sylvan lawns and unobstructed views of Little Traverse Bay. Seasonal flowers and gently waving flags add to these pleasantly inviting entranceways.

Wequetonsing (top)

Illinois businessmen and lawyers Henry Stryker III and Henry Brigham McClure founded *Weque*, as locals call it. Both were connected to the Jacob Bunn railroad dynasty. A resort within a resort, Weque is replete with colorful gardens, shaded walks and vacation homes, many passed down from generation to generation.

Bayside Beach (bottom)

The private beach in this resort community often teems with kids and adults alike. They frolic in the often-chilly waters and play along beaches whose width varies with the weather. Water-sports lovers glide by in kayaks, canoes and paddle boards. Colorful Adirondack chairs and water toys dot the sand.

Zoll Street Park and Beach *(top)*

Zoll Street Beach is one of Harbor Springs' smallest, and a favorite of families, sunbathers and dog owners. Avid swimmers often start their lake laps here along the waterfront, parallel to Wequetonsing. Seen in the distance are moored boats and the curve of Harbor Point, extending into Lake Michigan.

Sk8 Park Pickleball Courts *(bottom)*

Mirroring pickleball's meteoric growth in recent years, Harbor Springs now has several outdoor courts. This one plus a second are next to the skate park and adjacent to the Kosequat Park baseball field on Main Street. Players bring their own equipment and use is on a first-come, first-serve basis.

Ugotta Regatta (top)

More than 100 sailboats race on the bay's unpredictable waters during the annual Ugotta Regatta. Begun in 1961 and sponsored by Little Traverse Yacht Club, the challenging regatta draws thousands of spectators and occurs after the Chicago to Mackinac and Port Huron to Mackinac races in early July.

Little Traverse Yacht Club (bottom)

Founded in 1895, the Little Traverse Yacht Club is one of the oldest such clubs in the Midwest. Its home is a vintage, wood-frame structure on Bay Street. The yacht club sponsors the annual Ugotta Regatta, a jam-packed weekend of races and festivities. The club also holds sailing classes for kids.

Shopping District *(top and bottom)*

Ivy Parnasius opened Ivy Boutique on the first floor of this corner building in 2018 after moving to Northern Michigan from Colorado. The shop offers affordable women's clothing grouped by color, jewelry and accessories. It is one of many lining Main Street, the main artery in town also known as *M-119*.

Stafford's Pier Docks (above)

Poking out into the sometimes-calm waters of Harbor Springs, this large concrete pier provides a temporary berth for jaw-dropping yachts and sailboats from ports near and far. Visitors enjoy strolling the pier and linger on benches to ogle the immaculate vessels that are often staffed with uniformed crews.

Stafford's Pier Restaurant (right)

Once a speakeasy, Stafford's Pier Restaurant sits atop 75-foot pilings where the original *Pointer* boathouse formerly stood. Its seasonal outdoor deck faces the yacht basin. Inside, the Pier is decorated in spiffy nautical style. It is part of Stafford Hospitality, owner of the Perry Hotel, Bay View Inn and Weathervane restaurant.

State and Bay Street Corner *(top)*

Formerly Leahy's New York Hotel that featured a first-floor bowling alley, this red-brick building is now New York Restaurant. Owner and chef since 1977, Matt Bugera uses fresh local ingredients and homegrown herbs. Across the street is the circa-1894 Bar Harbor, known by locals as *Last Call*.

Tom's Mom's Cookies *(bottom)*

Whenever Tom's Mom's Cookies bakes their signature three-inch cookies, enticing aromas waft over Harbor Springs. This charming Victorian store, with a profuse garden and sometimes a long line out front, first opened in 1985. Owner Sheryl McCleery offers 20 different cookie types, all preservative-free.

Shopping District *(above and right)*

Harbor Springs bustles with brightly-hued shops, galleries, restaurants, bars and ice-cream purveyors, many housed in original buildings. Some stay open until 8 p.m. on soft summer evenings. Most are one-of-a-kind with regular customers on a first-name basis. A vintage clock adds to the town's old-time charm.

Farmer's Market (top)

Like Petoskey, Charlevoix and other towns, Harbor Springs hosts a Farmer's Market during spring and summer. Twice a week, the market offers a bounty of fresh, local produce, hand-milled soaps, yarn and French macaroons. Visitors enjoy live music and can stroll Main Street, pedestrian-only on market days.

Vintage Car Show (bottom)

Harbor Springs holds its annual Car Festival every August, usually at Zorn Park just off Little Traverse Bay. Displayed are more than 200 seldom-seen vehicles of all types—rat and hot rods, sports and muscle cars, vintage and classic wheels. Showing off one's car is free, as is the event itself.

Boyer Glassworks

Harry Boyer creates exquisite works of art from hand-blown glass at his State Street studio. Renowned for his splendid luminescent pumpkins, displayed at his gallery and Cross Village's Three Pines Studio, he and fellow artisan Lynn Dinning sell pumpkins in October at the Great Lakes Pumpkin Patch event.

Red Barn and Fields (top)

Barns and other buildings really pop out of the landscape when snow blankets the ground. The region gets an average 110 inches of the white stuff each winter. Flakes sometimes swirl as early as October and can fall as late as April. December and January are the snowiest months and April is known for its mud.

Leaden Skies Over Walloon (bottom)

While many regard Northern Michigan as a summertime destination, other seasons are rich with outdoor activities too. Walloon Lake displays the pellucid grayness that precedes ice. Once frozen over, cold-weather buffs skate, snowmobile and ice-boat on the lake. Avid ice-fishing anglers erect protective shanties.

Christmas in Harbor Springs (top)

Displaying a live tree on Main Street in front of Holy Childhood Church has been an annual event since 1915. A boat trailer hauls a 40-footer here, and the trunk is stabilized inside a manhole. One switch dramatically illuminates the tree and Main Street lights. Santa Claus arrives and the air resounds with carols.

Snow-skiing at Nub's Nob (bottom)

High atop hills overlooking Harbor Springs, Nub's Nob began in 1959 when Dorie and Nub Sarns opened with three trails and a chairlift. Today, it has 53 skiing and snowboarding runs. Michigan has more ski areas than any other state but New York. Other area ski resorts are Boyne Mountain and Boyne Highlands.

Bay View Porches (above and left)

Like Harbor Springs, Bay View Association is known as a quaint community of brightly painted Victorian homes with welcoming front porches. This vibrant arts and residential resort hugging the shore of Little Traverse Bay has 31 public buildings and 447 homes, many adorned with cottage names and flags. At left, the Kerby cottage, named *One of Life's Rewards*, proudly flies its University of Michigan flag.

Bay View Homes and Association
(above and right)

A picturesque community, Bay View began in 1875 when Methodist leaders formed a *chautauqua*, part of a larger educational and social movement where congregants gathered to worship, socialize and camp. People eventually built cottages and public buildings, and expanded cultural and entertainment offerings. This tradition still flourishes today. Bay View gained National Historic Landmark status in 1987.

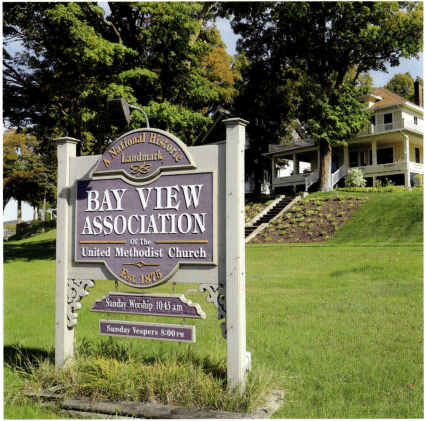

Gingerbread Details (above and left)

Many Bay View homes are built in the Victorian Queen Anne style, with brightly painted gingerbread trim, cupolas, towers, porches and other ornate details. Self-guided walking tours take visitors past historic buildings and down curving streets and alleys that meander through the land's natural terraces. The community sponsors occasional house tours during the summer.

Victorian Cottages *(above)*

Bay View residents often call their resort homes *cottages*, though many are hardly small. This painted Victorian lady atop a gentle knoll is one such imposing example. Typically not winterized, cottages are often inherited with ownership extending over generations. Proud residents give their cottages fanciful names and hang them on placards over front doors and porches.

Evelyn Hall *(right)*

Once housing the Women's Christian Temperance Union, Evelyn Hall was later used as a cooking school and lecture hall. Today, theater and music students rehearse here. Bay View lovingly restored the building in 1998. It is considered one of the finest examples of Queen Anne architecture in the state of Michigan.

Stafford's Bay View Inn (top)

Across from Bay View sits this gracious inn and restaurant with expansive water views. John Wesley Howard built it in 1886 and called it the Howard Inn, later known as Hotel Roselawn. It is owned by Stafford's Hospitality, as are the Pier in Harbor Springs, Petoskey's Perry Hotel and the Weathervane in Charlevoix.

Terrace Inn (bottom)

Step into the Terrace Inn and revisit the past. Decorated in Art Deco and Craftsman styles, the inn has 38 rooms and the 1911 Restaurant, which was named for the year William DeVol of Indiana built it. A long staircase leads down to Fair View Park and the sparkling bay beyond. The Inn is open year-round.

John M. Hall Auditorium *(top)*

Named for Bay View's longtime educational director, Hall Auditorium seats 1,400 for ecumenical worship and vesper concerts every Sunday during the season. Musical performances, as well as educational and entertainment events, are also staged here. Scholarship students stage a full-length opera each summer.

Bay View Recreation Club *(bottom)*

From toddlers to adults, the club offers something for everyone. Several tennis courts hug the bay's shoreline. It also has sailing and swimming lessons, crafts, games, yoga and more. Pickleball takes place at the Bay View Woods Courts. The community sponsors a day camp at Swift Field for kids ages 3-14.

Bay View Buildings

Built in 1876, the white frame building with its pagoda-style roof *(top right)* is Bay View's oldest. It was variously occupied by the secretary's office, an art studio and kids' clubhouse. A rustic Speaker's Stand, made from intertwined hemlock stumps, stood outside. Preachers and others orated here. The building on the left was the bookstore. Today, the two comprise Bay View's museum. The community also has its own post office and lawn croquet court. Epworth Hall *(bottom left)* has long housed members of Bay View's music faculty. The Campus Club *(bottom right)* offers an array of games, programs and social events for all ages.

Crouse Chapel

Aglow with luminous stained glass, this tiny chapel is named for former Bay View philanthropist Virginia Crouse. A Lima, Ohio native, Crouse summered at Bay View, where her grandparents first vacationed in 1895. Once the campus general store, it became a chapel in 1993 and seats 80 for ecumenical services and weddings.

Bay Harbor Yacht Club and Homes
(top and bottom)

Bay Harbor was once the site of the huge Petoskey Portland and later Penn-Dixie cement companies. Cement manufacturing flourished here, given the area's abundance of limestone and natural materials. Upon Penn-Dixie's bankruptcy, Detroit developer David V. Johnson bought its five miles of shoreline and 1,200 acres. A childhood vacationer in Northern Michigan, Johnson built a low-density, world-class resort with more than 500 homes, two hotels, a shopping district, restaurants, a deep-water marina and other amenities.

Bay Harbor From the Bay

Seen from Little Traverse Bay, these homes face both the bay and Bay Harbor Lake. Engineers created the lake when they detonated the cement plant in a gigantic dust and debris cloud. More than 2.5 billion gallons of Lake Michigan water rushed into the abyss and created a lake 80 feet at its deepest.

Bay Harbor Evening (top and bottom)

Each evening, the marina and shopping area take on a soft glow as the sun dips below the horizon. The marina underwent expansion in 2022 and now has 150 seasonal and transient boat slips. In Bay Harbor's compact shopping area on Main Street, buildings are emblazoned with names of the five Great Lakes.

Great Lakes Center for the Arts
(top and bottom)

Completed in 2018, this distinctive state-of-the-art performance venue was built by theater designers Fisher Dachs Associates and architects TowerPinkster and has become a significant addition to Northern Michigan's lively arts scene. The auditorium seats 525 and has ten, upper-level private boxes. Open year-round, the center offers a robust entertainment roster of theater, music, dance, and film. Educational programs in the arts are also offered. A chic lounge, rooftop terrace overlooking the bay and patio enrich the social experience.

Bay Harbor Homes and Lake

Many of Bay Harbor's grand Victorian-style homes sit on reclaimed spits of land. The sparkling bay beyond is their panoramic backyard. Some have docks where residents park boats and other water toys. Bay Harbor remains one of the largest abandoned industrial sites in North America ever to be repurposed.

Bay Harbor Village and Ferry

Locals say the two imposing buildings of the Bay Harbor Village *(top)* resemble grounded cruise ships. Shops, restaurants, condos and the Bay Harbor Village Hotel & Conference Center are located here. The revived Little Traverse Ferry *(bottom)* runs daily in-season from Bay Harbor and Petoskey to Harbor Springs.

Bay Harbor Shops *(above and left)*

Bay Harbor's compact shopping district is anchored on one end by the Bay Harbor Village Hotel & Conference Center, recognized by its unusual porthole balconies and mansard roof. A first-floor restaurant at lake level offers indoor and outdoor seating in season. Tents are often erected for weddings and other events.

The Inn at Bay Harbor *(top)*

Owned by Boyne Resorts, the sprawling Inn at Bay Harbor pays homage to the area's once-vibrant inn-keeping trade of the late 19th century. Part of Marriott's Autograph Collection, and reminiscent of the Grand Hotel on Mackinac Island, this red-roofed edifice has 105 rooms, cottages, a spa, beachfront and restaurant.

Quarry to Luxury Resort *(bottom)*

One would never suspect that Bay Harbor was once a cement plant and quarries. A sandy beach now hugs the bay, the Inn at Bay Harbor and its outdoor pool, deck and lawn looming in the distance. In warmer months, the verdant lawn in front beckons with croquet, bocce and whimsical large-scale chess.

From Quarry to Luxury Resort
(top and bottom)

Single-family homes and townhouses perch atop the shale face of a former Bay Harbor cement plant quarry. Occasionally, water trickles from the rocks, soaking the pedestrian and bike path that borders the cliff. The Bay Harbor marquee along US 31 often displays upcoming events.

Gatehouse and Golf

Gatehouses stand guard at several Bay Harbor communities. Golf reigns supreme here. Edging the bay are three, 9-hole Arthur Hills designed courses—the Quarry, Links, and Preserve. These often-blustery links are dubbed *the Pebble Beach of the Midwest*. Boyne Resorts owns the stunning clubhouses and courses.

Walloon Lake Country Club *(top)*

Perched atop a gentle rise on the North Arm, the private Walloon Lake Country Club first opened its doors in 1904. Membership now numbers 275. Like so many other places in Northern Michigan, it is open seasonally, from May 1 to October 15. Many members travel from elsewhere on the lake by boat.

Country Club Fariway *(bottom)*

Designed by Bruce Matthews III and Mike DeVries, this 18-hole course overlooking Walloon Lake is fast and hilly. Additional amenities include tennis and pickleball courts plus golf and tennis pros to sharpen skills. Sailing, swimming and other activities abound for kids. Lunch and dinner are available seasonally.

Bear River Weir *(top and bottom)*

Walloon Lake flows into the Bear River at The Foot. A *weir*, or small dam built across a river, controls water flow from the lake. The usually easy-flowing Bear River slices through farm fields and forests as it makes its way to Petoskey and Little Traverse Bay. Paddleboards, kayaks and canoes often dot the river.

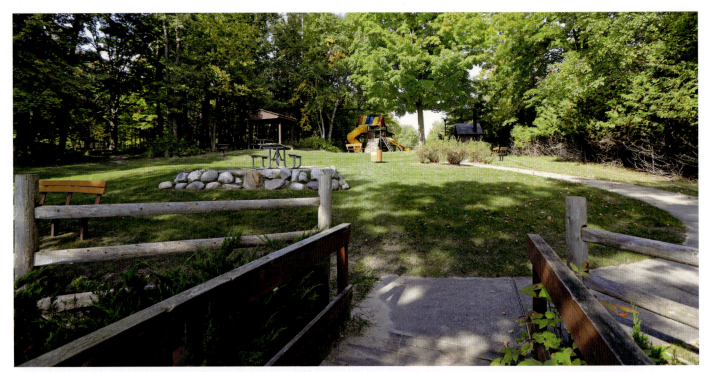

Resort Township Park (top)

A pocket park at the end of Resort Pike, the land descends to water's edge via a rustic stairway. Carved from glaciers long ago, Walloon Lake opens up at the bottom, beckoning visitors with a place to skip rocks, wade and soak up rays. The park has a playground, picnic benches, grills and restrooms.

Barrel Back Restaurant (bottom)

Named for an iconic Woody boat with a rounded transom resembling a floating barrel, The Foot's year-round Barrel Back Restaurant provides open-air seating and an outdoor bar packed with patrons on warm days. Inside, garage doors roll open to let in the breeze. Tommy's water-sports shop is downstairs.

Walloon Lake Parks *(top and bottom)*

From a sandy Melrose Township Park beach at the Foot, Walloon opens to a vast aquamarine panorama. This calm spot, overlooking Michigan's 26th largest lake, is tailor-made for water sports and relaxation. The park continues across M 75, with a playground, gazebo, picnic area and volleyball court near the Bear River.

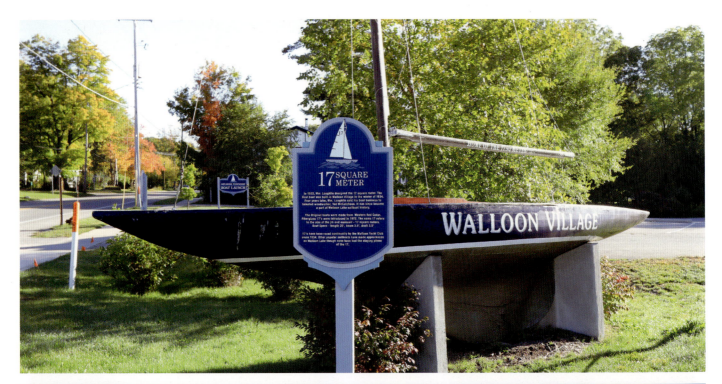

17 Sailboat (top)

A Walloon icon, this 17 replica stands guard at the Foot. William Loughlin built the first 17 in 1934 from western red cedar and later sold his business to local woodworker Ted McCutcheon. The number 17 refers to the sleek vessel's 17 square meters of sail. Fiberglass models first appeared in the 1970s.

Tommy's (bottom)

Developer Jonathan Borisch, a former defense contractor, is largely credited with rebuilding the Foot, where he spent summers as a boy. Borisch and son Matt transformed this sleepy hamlet into a regional mecca, building Hotel Walloon, shops, the Barrel Back restaurant and Tommy's, a water sports retail shop.

Hotel Walloon (top)

Built in 2015, the luxury 32-room Hotel Walloon recalls a bygone era. It was voted one of *Travel + Leisure's* top 10 midwestern resorts in 2022, ranking it higher than any in Michigan. The hotel has a private bar, billiards and fitness rooms and outdoor whirlpool. Weddings and other events often are held here.

Shoppers Dock (bottom)

Energetic red-clad dock attendants scurry about the numerous Foot docks, helping boaters and shoppers dock their watercraft and fuel up their tanks. The Foot is one of two places on Walloon where boaters can refuel. The other is at Bear Cove Marina on the western shore of the West Arm.

Walloon Lake Docks (top)

The 60-slip docks at the Foot poke into the lake on a tranquil summer's day. Boaters can easily dock to take advantage of the Foot's Barrel Back restaurant, shops, ice cream parlor, coffee shop, post office, public library and other amenities. Wallooners often travel to and fro by boat, weather permitting.

Walloon Lake Inn (bottom)

This historic restaurant was originally Fern Cottage. Built in 1891, it was near where passenger boats steamed up and down the lake to pick up vacationers. Save for Hotel Walloon nearby, the lake's era of fine hotels is largely past. The inn, open year-round, offers superb lake views and gourmet cuisine.

Walloon Sailors (above)

Walloon Lake Country Club offers sailing lessons each summer on the North Arm for kids ages 7 and up. These Walloon Sailors are often spotted in one of 14 centerboard-equipped dinghies called *Optimists*, nicknamed *Optis*. The club sponsors an annual parent-and-child regatta where moms and dads crew for their kids.

Sculpture at Walloon Lake Foot (right)

A striking stone sculpture stands in the park next to the Barrel Back. It depicts teachings from the Seven Grandfathers, a legend from the Ojibway, Odawa and Potawatomi Native American tribes who first settled this land. The indentations represent traditional tribal family values such as wisdom, love and honesty.

Walloon North Arm (above)

The North Arm, one of three, is Walloon's most shallow, making its water warmer than anywhere else on the lake. Area sandbars can cause boaters to run aground. Walloon Lake Country Club is on the arm's eastern shore. The arm can be viewed spreading out below from high atop US 131 near Coveyou Scenic Farm Market.

Walloon Lake Village (top)

Glaciers carved the lake's unique shape, which some liken to a paint blotch. It is fed by springs bubbling up from a limestone-rich bottom, creating sudden warm and cool spots. Previously called Bear Lake, then Talcott, it became Walloon circa 1900—a name derived from Belgians who settled at its northern end.

Randall's Point (bottom)

Protruding into the main part of Walloon is Randall's Point, once owned by Bo Randall, founder of Randall Made Knives. Randall was also Hemingway's hunting buddy. The 15-acre property, with its log cabins and barn, sits back from the lake. Boaters anchor here to sunbathe and frolic in the shallow water.

Fishing on the Lake *(above and left)*

Fishing is wildly popular, especially in spring and fall when the water is cool, docks are not yet in and seasonal residents have not yet arrived. Anglers navigate the lake in boats simple and high-tech. They land small-mouth bass, northern pike, perch, walleye and rainbow and lake trout, the latter two stocked.

Eagle Island *(opposite top)*

Actually a peninsula, Eagle Island helps form The Narrows, a waterway between the West Arm and Main Basin. It was once home to several kids' camps: Hemlock, Huntington and Sherwood, plus the Eagle Island Resort, which burned in 1919. The West Arm's Camp Daggett is the oldest Walloon sleep-over camp.

Main Basin *(opposite bottom)*

Walloon Lake is 1.3 miles at its widest. Bisecting parts of the lake is the boundary between Charlevoix and Emmet counties. The lake is nine miles long and has more than 30 miles of pristine shoreline. The shallow and wildlife-rich Mill Pond, until recently called Mud Lake, is at the West Arm's northern tip.

Windemere

Arriving via train and steamboat from their Oak Park, Ill., home, Ernest Hemingway's family vacationed here. His descendants still live in this shorefront cottage, which is not open to the public. He and first wife Hadley Richardson honeymooned at Windemere in 1921, visiting only once after his nuptials.

Windemere (top)

Hemingway learned to hunt, fish, and possibly carouse here. Built in 1899, Windemere retains original furnishings and memorabilia, including a penciled chart showing the writer's height changes. Mother Grace often escaped her large family, paddling a canoe to where she had a small cabin.

Hemingway Statue (bottom)

Hemingway's 1953 Pulitzer-Prize winning *The Old Man and the Sea* inspired artist George Lundeen to create this bronze sculpture at the Foot's village park. Hemingway is depicted with his beloved fishing rod and one of his six-toed cats, whose descendants still occupy his Key West, Fla., compound.

Hiking Trails *(top and bottom right)*

Gorgeous trails traverse Northern Michigan and the Walloon area is no exception. Most are well-marked for hikers, cross-country skiers and snowshoers. Open since 2019, the 122-acre Pioneer Trails honors early homesteaders. In spring, hillsides abound with white and pink trillium, actually a wild orchid.

American Bald Eagle *(bottom left)*

These regal predators glide over Walloon, often close to shore. They nest in lakeside trees and return to feed their eaglets. Because fish are eagles' main food, the raptors lurk near water. Watching them soar, then plunge into the lake to spear a meal, is a sight to behold. An eagle's wing-span can reach seven feet.

Walloon Lake Association and Conservancy Nature Preserves *(opposite)*

The advocacy group stewards 51 preserves covering 2,200 acres. Recognized by green signs, the preserves range from tiny to 153 acres with 24 miles of trails, streams and abundant wildlife. Begun 110 years ago, the association has over 1,000 members and sponsors fun and educational events.

17 Sailboat

The sleek 17 sailboat was built specifically for Walloon's tricky and often powerful winds. With its fixed fin keel and 25-foot length, the two-person 17 is quite stable, rarely capsizing in howling winds. About 40 17s still exist, half the newer fiberglass variety. They are found moored on buoys near their owners' docks.

Camp Michigania (top)

Open to University of Michigan alumni, the 377-acre Camp Michigania sits on the former site of the Sherwood and Huntington summer camps. Opened in 1963, it has grown exponentially and is now year-round. Guests stay in rustic cabins, dine in a cavernous mess hall and participate in an abundance of activities.

Kayaking (bottom)

Kayaking is popular, especially when Walloon is placid. The West Arm's Camp Daggett hosts the annual *Kayak for a Cause* each July. Funds are raised for Daggett's Adventure Education Center and other programs. Paddlers depart Bear Cove Marina, glide around the West Arm and end with lunch at Daggett.

Sailboat Racing on Walloon Lake (top)

The first recorded sailboat race on Walloon took place in 1909. The Walloon Yacht Club racing season, from late June through early August, rotates from the Foot to the North and West arms. Races, held Tuesday evenings and weekend afternoons, are breathtaking, especially when spinnakers unfurl to catch the wind.

Water Sports (bottom)

Sports on and in the water abound on Walloon and other Northern Michigan lakes, from water- and jet-skiing, wake-surfing and tubing to pontoon boat cruises, paddleboarding, swimming, sailing and more. Tommy's, Bear Cove Marina and other local shops offer boats and water-sports equipment of all kinds.

Vintage Wooden Boats *(top and bottom)*

On many a nice day, the deep-throated thrum of vintage wooden boats echoes across Walloon. These majestic boats are truly a sight to behold. Each summer, in a stunning parade of rumbling engines and rolling waves, dozens of Walloon *Woody* owners pilot boats to the Foot, where spectators can ogle these classics.

WALLOON LAKE | 111

Paddleboarding (above)

Stand-up paddleboards, or *SUPs*, provide enthusiasts with an accessible hybrid sport that blends kayaking and surfing. Paddleboarding first sprang to prominence in the early 2000s, with boards becoming increasingly high-tech, stable and lightweight. Walloon is often peppered with paddleboards, some carting dogs and little kids when the water is calm.

Tubing on Walloon Lake (left)

Another accessible water sport, tubing attracts people of all ages. Motor boats pull inflated donuts and other shapes behind them, attached by a rope tow. Kids and adults climb atop these devices for an exhilarating spin on the lake. Shouts of delight from tubers are a common sound on Walloon Lake.

Dock Time *(above and right)*

Whether lounging and laughing or frolicking in the crystalline water, Walloon's signature docks are a big part of what makes lake life so special. Removed as temperatures cool and reassembled in warmer weather, many display dockside flags of colleges and universities, snapping and flapping on windy days.

Milky Way (opposite)

Star-gazing is a favorite Up North pastime. Little air and light pollution allow the Milky Way to be seen creasing the sky on many a Walloon evening. Gazers frequently spot shooting stars, and in fall and spring can see the huge Pleiades star cluster. Lucky viewers sometimes see the Northern Lights too.

Fireside (top)

Fire pits and bonfires are popular on Walloon and other lakes. Cottagers often make oozy, rich s'mores, imbibe and gather close to the flames on cool nights. Communities and residents need little reason to set off fireworks, the most spectacular over-water displays occuring during Fourth of July celebrations.

Sunset at the Foot (bottom)

Looking west toward Lake Michigan from the docks at Walloon's Foot, the pellucid waters mirror a flaming sky above. With good reason, the region is often called *The Land of the Million-Dollar Sunsets*. Lakes are everywhere, and the ubiquitous presence of water causes dramatic reflections in both lake and sky.

Charlevoix Clock (top)

Called *Charlevoix the Beautiful*, this jewel is replete with picturesque details. Charlevoix is named for French explorer Pierre de Charlevoix, who traveled here in the 18th century. Midwesterners flocked north via trains and steamships. Old-guard communities still exist, like the Belvedere, Chicago and Sequanota clubs.

Lake Charlevoix Aerial View (bottom)

The funnel-shaped lake is Michigan's third-largest by surface area. Its two lengthy arms make its 60-mile shoreline far longer than any other Michigan inland lake. Given its direct connection to Lake Michigan through the Pine River Channel, Charlevoix's water level fluctuates with lakes Michigan and Huron.

Lake Charlevoix (top)

The cerulean blue lake is 2.5 miles at its widest and 122 feet at its deepest. Water-sports fans flock here in warmer weather to sail, water-ski, kayak, powerboat, fish, swim and indulge in other lake-life pursuits. Nearby marinas offer boat tours plus private and sunset charters that often include Lake Michigan.

Weathervane and Walkway (bottom)

A fenced walkway leads west toward the lighthouse and Lake Michigan beyond. The Weathervane, a Stafford's Hospitality eatery, was a grist mill until the mid-1950s when Charlevoix builder Earl Young converted it, adding a limestone exterior with Onaway stone trim and a spectacular nine-ton glacial boulder fireplace.

Beaver Island Ferry (top)

The island's lifeblood, the ferry departs from Charlevoix to make a two-hour, 32-mile trek with water views as far as the eye can see. Beaver Island is Lake Michigan's largest and has 600 year-round residents. It offers beaches, forests and a harbor. It is best known as the former home of a Latter Day Saints kingdom.

Ironton Ferry (bottom)

The scenic car and passenger ferry connects Lake Charlevoix's Ironton Narrows and South Arm. Begun in 1876 and once pulled by horses, the ferry today operates by cables and is one of the shortest in the U.S. A ride takes all of five minutes. The ferry runs from mid-April through late November, weather permitting.

Pine River Channel Drawbridge (top)

Looking west toward Lake Michigan and along the Pine River Channel, the Charlevoix drawbridge opens on the hour and half-hour for taller boats. Watching it ascend and descend delights many a Northern Michigan visitor. At night, the 74-year-old bridge puts on a dramatic light show with 3,000 LED bulbs.

Pine River Channel (bottom)

The narrow channel connects Round and Charlevoix lakes to Lake Michigan. In the 19th century, Pine River clogged with boulders and logs, making passage impossible without portaging. Laborers cleaned and straightened it. Immediately, maritime activity boomed in Charlevoix, and still does to this day.

Boulder Park *(top and bottom)*

Charlevoix builder Earl Young developed Boulder Park southwest of town on land bordering Lake Michigan's shore. Given his aversion to grid-like neighborhoods, he created irregularly shaped parcels and curved roads. Homes were built largely from stone and he later marked the development with a forty-ton boulder.

Lake Michigan Lighthouse and Walk

At the end of the Pine River pier stands a red steel lighthouse, which replaced a wooden version in 1948. Its fog bell is now silent but a beacon still shines. The city of Charlevoix owns the lighthouse, one of 129 in Michigan. Pedestrians can walk to the end of the pier. The lighthouse itself is shuttered.

Boulder Park Homes *(top)*

Earl Young built four commercial buildings and 26 homes in Charlevoix, using limestone, fieldstone and boulders from throughout the area. With wavy eaves and cedar-shake roofs, these unique homes blend into their surroundings. Named for their mushroom-like appearance, they are also known as *gnome* or *Hobbit houses*.

Mushroom Houses *(bottom)*

Without the use of blueprints, Earl Young designed homes to fit the land. Most are small but others, such as the dramatic Thatch Roof House *(bottom right),* are commanding. Many Young houses have low ceilings because the builder himself was diminutive. Guided exterior tours are offered occasionally.

East Park and Amphitheatre *(top)*

Hugging Round Lake and the 65-slip Charlevoix marina, East Park and its distinctive amphitheatre, with superb natural acoustics, are across from the town's main shopping district. An interactive water fountain cools and delights children on sultry days. The park also has a trout pond with rushing water features.

Ferry Beach at Lake Charlevoix *(bottom)*

Ferry Beach is one of several public beaches on the lake. It offers two separate swimming areas, where the bottom is sandy and the water is warmer and usually calmer than Lake Michigan. Close to the city boat slip, it also has stand-up paddleboard and kayak rentals, plus a playground and restrooms.

Little Traverse Wheelway (top)

Swaths of the wheelway between Bay Harbor and Charlevoix closely edge Lake Michigan. A 26-mile paved path for pedestrians and cyclists, the wheelway offers stunning and unimpeded lake views along much of its length. The largely flat path is home to many bike and run/walk races each year.

John Cross Fisheries (bottom)

A third-generation fish store on Round Lake, this year-round market sells fresh and smoked Great Lake fish, and other seafood types, to retail customers, local restaurants and markets. Customers queue up for whitefish, perch, walleye and other specialties. Its white clapboard shop is a beloved Charlevoix institution.

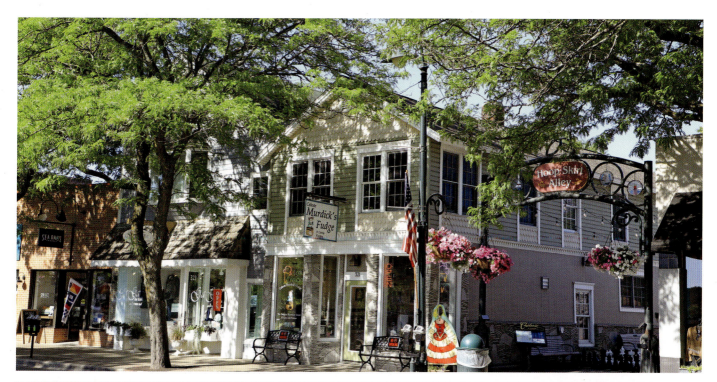

Charlevoix Shopping (top)

A city of 3,200 year-round residents, Charlevoix teems with seasonal visitors. State Street, the main drag, is lined with largely one-of-a-kind boutiques, restaurants, and microbreweries. Pictured is Murdick's Fudge, where spectators can watch as workers cool fudge and form it into blocks on marble tables.

Cherry Republic (bottom)

Charlevoix has one of Cherry Republic's six Michigan stores, whose mantra is, *Life, Liberty, Beaches & Pie*. The shop sells more than 200 irresistible cherry-based products ranging from chocolate-covered cherries and cherry beer to salsas and nut mixes, all celebrating the region's Montmorency tart cherries.

Round Lake and Marina (top)

The 77-slip Round Lake marina at Charlevoix's East Park is a lively place to stroll and ogle the boats. It has floating docks, a boaters' lounge, laundry facilities and restrooms, plus diesel and gasoline sales, marine repairs and supplies. Ringing Round Lake are historic boathouses and homes, several by Earl Young.

Historic Mural (bottom)

In 2015, artist Katherine Larson painted her *Charlevoix the Beautiful* tableau on aluminum at her Ann Arbor studio. The colorful mural was then installed on a lengthy Central Drug brick wall facing West Clinton Street. Five sections start in 1910 and end with a tribute to Earl Young's famous mushroom houses.

Charlevoix Train Station

The historic, gabled train station at Lake Charlevoix's Depot Beach is a reminder of a bygone era when trains reigned supreme. Owned by the Charlevoix Historical Society, it was once a stop on the Chicago & West Michigan line between Grand Rapids and Petoskey. Trains first chugged into Charlevoix in 1892.

 **Tom Barrat** is a photographer specializing in travel, wildlife and architecture. With a portfolio of images from all over the United States and 35 countries, he is a contributing photographer to multiple stock agencies, as well as his own website. More than half of Tom's 80,000 images have been sold internationally and downloaded for use on websites, magazine ads, newspapers, corporate reports, travel books, and other print and digital media.

Tom and his wife, Sherry, have been vacationing in Northern Michigan for the last 10 years, and are the happy owners of a home on historic Walloon Lake. *Up North Michigan* shares the charm and beauty of Walloon Lake and surrounding communities.

Tom's exquisite photography is also featured in two editions of *Chicago, A Photographic Portrait* by Twin Lights Publishers. He brings that same passion to *Up North Michigan*. Visit TomBarratPhotography.com to learn more.

 **Sarah Moran Martin** is a writer and editor for whom Northern Michigan is woven into her life. Once a *Kiplinger Washington Letter* editor, she then wrote for the *Daily Local News* outside Philadelphia, where she now lives with husband Tom. She also freelanced for *Washingtonian Magazine* and various other newspapers and magazines. Writing has always been her passion—almost as important as her love for all things Northern Michigan.

A native of suburban Detroit, Sarah and her family traveled every summer to Petoskey, where her mother grew up. In 1973, Sarah's parents built a cottage overlooking Walloon Lake's spectacular West Arm, a home now owned by Sarah, brother Jeff and their families. She spends as much time as she can Up North with her husband Tom, three grown sons and their families, where they delight in lake life, the region's natural beauty and its rich cultural heritage.

Contact Sarah at semoran219@gmail.com.